THE HYPERLINKED LIFE

FRAMES
BARNA GROUP

THE HYPERLINKED LIFE

Live with Wisdom in an Age of Information Overload

JUN YOUNG & DAVID KINNAMAN
RE/FRAME BY BRANDON SCHULZ

ZONDERVAN®

ZONDERVAN

The Hyperlinked Life
Copyright © 2013 by Barna Group

This title is also available as a Zondervan ebook.
Visit www.zondervan.com/ebooks.

This title is also available in a Zondervan audio edition.
Visit www.zondervan.fm.

Requests for information should be addressed to:

Zondervan, *Grand Rapids, Michigan 49530*

ISBN 978-0-310-43320-0 (softcover)

Published in association with the literary agency of The Fedd Agency, Inc, 401 Ranch Road 620 South, Suite 350c, Austin, TX 78734.

Cover design and interior graphics: Amy Duty
Interior design: Kate Mulvaney

Printed in the United States of America

13 14 15 16 17 18 /DCI/ 18 17 16 15 14 13 12 11 10 9 8 7 6 5 4 3 2 1

CONTENTS

19:8993

WHY YOU NEED FRAMES

....

These days, you probably find yourself with less time than ever.

Everything seems like it's moving at a faster pace — except your ability to keep up.

Somehow, you are weighed down with more obligations than you have ever had before.

Life feels more complicated. More complex.

If you're like most people, you probably have lots of questions about how to live a life that matters. You feel as though you have more to learn than can possibly be learned. But with smaller chunks of time and more sources of information than ever before, where can you turn for real insight and livable wisdom?

Barna Group has produced this series to examine the complicated issues of life and to help you live more meaningfully. We call it FRAMES — like a good set of eyeglasses that help you see the world more clearly . . . or a work of art perfectly hung that invites you to look more closely . . . or a building's skeleton, the part that is most essential to its structure.

The FRAMES Season 1 collection provides thoughtful and concise, data-driven and visually appealing insights for anyone who wants a more faith-driven and fulfilling life. In each FRAME we couple new cultural analysis from our team at Barna with an essay from leading voices in the field, providing information and ideas for you to digest in a more easily consumed number of words.

After all, it's a fast-paced world, full of words and images vying for your attention. Most of us have a number of half-read or "read someday" books on our shelves. But each FRAME aims to give you the essential information and real-life application behind one of today's most crucial trends in less than one-quarter the length of most books. These are big ideas in small books — designed so you truly can read less but know more. And the infographics and ideas in this FRAME are intended for share-ability. So read it, then find someone to "frame" with these ideas and keep the conversation going (see "Share This Frame" on page 88).

Furthermore, each FRAME brings a distinctly Christian point of view to today's trends. In times of uncertainty, people look for guides. And we believe the Christian community is trying to make sense of the dramatic social changes happening around us.

Over the past thirty years, Barna Group has built a reputation as a trusted analyst of religion and culture. We offer cultural discernment for the Christian community by thoughtful analysts who care enough to tell the truth about what's really happening in today's society.

So sit back, but not for long. With FRAMES we invite you to read less and know more.

DAVID KINNAMAN
FRAMES, executive producer
president / Barna Group

ROXANNE STONE
FRAMES, general editor
vice president / Barna Group

Learn more at www.barnaframes.com.

F R A M E S

TITLE	20 and Something	Becoming Home	Fighting for Peace	Greater Expectations
PURPOSE	Have the Time of Your Life (And Figure It All Out Too)	Adoption, Foster Care, and Mentoring – Living Out God's Heart for Orphans	Your Role in a Culture Too Comfortable with Violence	Succeed (and Stay Sane) in an On-Demand, All-Access, Always-On Age
AUTHOR	David H. Kim	Jedd Medefind	Carol Howard Merritt & Tyler Wigg-Stevenson	Claire Diaz-Ortiz
KEY TREND	27% of young adults have clear goals for the next 5 years	62% of Americans believe Christians have a responsibility to adopt	47% of adults say they're less comfortable with violence than 10 years ago	42% of people are unhappy with their work/life balance

PERFECT FOR SMALL GROUP DISCUSSION

FRAMES Season 1: DVD
FRAMES Season 1: The Complete Collection

READ LESS.
KNOW MORE.

The Hyperlinked Life	Multi-Careering	Sacred Roots	Schools in Crisis	Wonder Women
Live with Wisdom in an Age of Information Overload	Do Work that Matters at Every Stage of Your Journey	Why Church Still Matters	They Need Your Help (Whether You Have Kids or Not)	Navigating the Challenges of Motherhood, Career, and Identity
Jun Young & David Kinnaman	Bob Goff	Jon Tyson	Nicole Baker Fulgham	Kate Harris
71% of adults admit they're overwhelmed by information	75% of adults are looking for ways to live a more meaningful life	51% of people don't think it's important to attend church	46% of Americans say public schools are worse than 5 years ago	72% of women say they're stressed

#BarnaFrames

www.barnaframes.com

BEFORE YOU READ

....

- Take a guess—how much time do you think you spend looking at a screen?

- How many times, on average, would you say you check your phone in a given day?

- Do you ever feel overwhelmed with how much information comes at you? Do you ever find all that information actually gets in the way of making a decision?

- What is the first word that comes to your mind to describe how you feel when you leave your phone behind for any length of time?

- Where do you get most of your news and information?

- How often (if ever) do you intentionally take a break from your digital devices?

- What three words would you use to describe "life today"?

barnaframes.com

THE HYPERLINKED LIFE

Live with Wisdom in an Age of Information Overload

INFOGRAPHICS

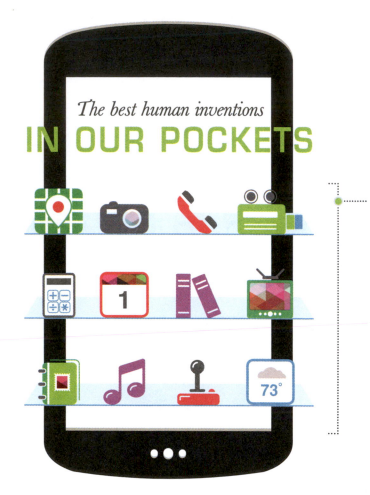

The best human inventions

IN OUR POCKETS

It's All Here!

Map / Camera / Telephone / Video Camera /
Calculator / Calendar / Encyclopedia / Television /
Photo Album / Music Player / Video Game Console / Weather Forecast

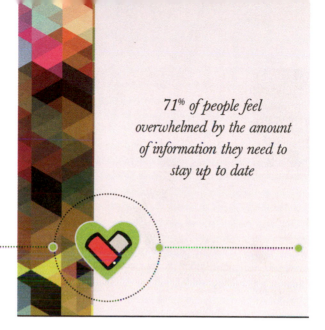

71% of people feel overwhelmed by the amount of information they need to stay up to date

I <3 MY CELL PHONE

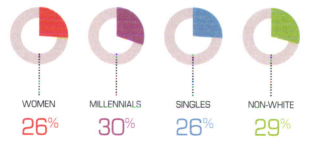

WOMEN	MILLENNIALS	SINGLES	NON-WHITE
26%	30%	26%	29%

And why wouldn't you? Part news anchor, part game console, part friendship network, and all convenience, that sleek gadget is basically an extra appendage. No wonder nearly one out of three adults say they love their cell phone. Of course, *love* is a strong word … and it's not far from turning an object into an idol. So while the cell phone brings the world to your fingertips, it's worth remembering the created thing is still just a *thing*.

LOL/ JK /
ROTFLUTS/
BTW/ BRB/
IRL/ THX/
ZOMG/ PLS
TTYL8R/ :)

42%

Millennials

36%

All adults

"When a text or message comes in, I usually stop what I'm doing to check it"

LOL all you want, but what's that text distracting you from in real life? Driving? Good conversation? An important conference call? The cookies burning in the oven? BRB, OK?

49%
Millennials

35%
All adults

"I think my personal electronics sometimes separate me from other people"

Our gadgets have added a lot to the world—an ability to be present in the moment probably isn't one of them. So go ahead, put the phone in your pocket and try some old-fashioned eye contact.

THE HYPERLINKED LIFE

Live with Wisdom in an Age of Information Overload

FRAMEWORK

BY BARNA GROUP

In the past fifteen years a revolution has taken place. You know about it because you've lived through it, but you may have missed its profound implications. Everyone's heard of the digital revolution, but this is so much more. It's the knowledge revolution.

Here is what this revolution looks like:

Not so long ago, we had to wait for information about our world to come to us. Books and other print items were among the first media that collected and distributed information in a relevant package for humans. Then came radio and television — electronic media that helped satiate human beings' thirst for more immediate knowledge. But all the media thus far have the disadvantage of being limited to bursts of information packaged for the largest possible audience. In other words, the information we gain via television and radio and newspapers is knowledge for mass consumption.

We still have access to information produced for mass consumption. But the knowledge revolution — with information now available through interconnected digital devices such as smartphones, tablets, and computers — is about *personalized* knowledge. It's not simply information for the masses; it's customized, personalized, on-demand information.

How the knowledge revolution is information — with you at the center of the universe.

The knowledge revolution is

- instant access to information about anything that interests you.

- finding ratings and directions to a restaurant when you're vacationing on a remote Pacific island.

- sports scores whenever your favorite team pops into your brain.

- customized spelling assistance for the words *you* have a hard time with.

- downloading that one song when you want it (and finding out what that one song is with just a remembered fragment of the chorus).

- going online to learn about health conditions as you experience them.

- knowing enough about your genetic history to make informed decisions about your medical future.

- discovering a new viewpoint on faith or spirituality when you're searching for it (or finding the specific Bible verse you're looking for, in multiple translations — again, when you need it).

- learning about where you travel — mapping the best routes, comparing customer ratings for destinations, and even previewing the sites on a digital street-view level.

- having a question enter your gray matter — about local weather, stock prices, breaking news, surf levels, or vegan recipes—and then satisfying that curiosity with a few clicks of a mouse or swipes of a finger.

The knowledge revolution is the rise of the *hyperlinked* life: access to what we want to know when we want to know it. Living in such a world requires a certain amount of adaptation. We had to adapt to the Industrial Age, and we will adapt to the Information Age. But we have to recognize there are both pitfalls and potential in adapting to this new world—a world in which we are all hyperlinked.

Being hyperlinked changes every aspect of our lives—and often for the better

How so?

- We can work from anywhere and at any time. We are not limited to working for companies that are in our own city, state, or even on the same continent where we live. Of course, such possibilities create expectations of being always available and always "on."

- The goal of education is no longer to impart information, which can be accessed through any Internet connection. Rather, it is to develop the skills to use this information. And formal schooling—like work—can be done remotely and without a set schedule.

- Social relationships can be maintained without regard for geographic boundaries or time differences. Talking online with a family member on the next continent

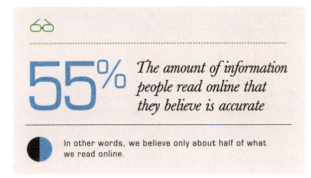

55%

The amount of information people read online that they believe is accurate

In other words, we believe only about half of what we read online.

feels just the same as talking online with a family member across the street.

- We can make better decisions — about products we want to purchase, companies we might work for, and what kind of dog best fits our lifestyle. We can even use this knowledge to anticipate our own genetic destiny, like actress Angelina Jolie did in 2013 when she opted to have a double mastectomy based on information about her genetic makeup that suggested a hazardously high likelihood of breast cancer in her future.

- "News" is now highly personal and highly collaborative. Think about your Twitter feed: the location of a favorite food truck, an update about your sister's recent run, then a friend's re-tweet of an article on the health benefits of coffee, and a breaking news tweet from an international publication on an uprising in the Middle East. There is no longer a hierarchy for information, and everyone's news "feels" unique and personalized: an amalgamation of friends, RSS feeds, emails, blogs, and tweets.

- Our churches are impacted. Consider what the local church provides: Bible teaching, inspiring sermons, Christian fellowship, a place to serve, and a time of worship. Now we can get Bible teaching and inspiring sermons from a "celebrity" pastor's podcast; we can "attend" church services online; we can receive Christian fellowship from Facebook; we volunteer at a local nonprofit; and we can worship with our Christian Pandora channel.

The benefits of the knowledge revolution are, of course, significant. The majority of those surveyed (55%) say there is joy in learning new things, and many (29%) feel the extra information gives them more control over the decisions they make. A significant minority (41%) say they have greater confidence in their decisions with this kind of access. But such access comes with a price too. As Ecclesiastes 1:18 says, "The more knowledge, the more grief."

Being hyperlinked changes every aspect of our lives — and often *not* for the better

Costs can come in the form of emotional, mental, physical, and, perhaps, spiritual tolls:

An Emotional Toll: Although few of us might choose to go back to an age without Google, we often feel overwhelmed by it all. In fact, more than seven out of ten adults (71%) admit to being overwhelmed by the amount of information they need to stay up to date—and they do not even totally trust what information they *do* get online. American adults (55%) admit to only believing about half of what they read online. A quarter of Americans (23%) say they *love* their phone. Which may explain why four in ten of them (40%) check it as their first act of each new day and 27% keep checking it at least once every waking hour after that. In addition, there can be an emotional toll from reading yet another real-life tragedy or suffering the effects of unrealistic expectations about how grand or posh or noticeable our lives are "supposed" to be.

A Mental Toll: More than half of Americans (54%) think they actually have *too much* information, and one in six (59%) say all that information can

The negative impact of
INFO OVERLOAD

54% *All adults*   56% *Millennials*

"There are times when I think I have too much information"

get in the way of making a decision. Nearly four in ten adults (36%) stop everything and check their phones whenever a new text or message comes in. About the same number (34%) say they get anxious when they forget to take their phone with them or the battery dies. Almost half (46%) would struggle to go without the Internet for longer than one day.

A Social Toll: Just over one third of all adults (35%) and nearly half of those under forty (47%) admit their personal electronics sometimes separate them from other people. The social sciences tell us there is no real substitute for in-person, face-to-face interaction. Yet, our social interaction is trending increasingly toward cyberspace than physical space.

A Spiritual Toll: And there may be a spiritual toll yet to come. In some ways, we are building a digital "Tower of Babel": a collaborative project to bring unity and enlightenment to our species. What dangers come with such godlike knowledge?

The genie, however, is out of the bottle. We are not going back to an era when we had to memorize facts or formulas to have them at our fingertips, when friends weren't available to us 24/7, and when activism couldn't be done in 140 characters or less.

The hyperlinked life is here to stay. So let's take a look at some of the data and trends that are producing this new iWorld. More important, let's take a look at what it means for God's people to thrive and bear witness to something greater than ourselves and the plethora of information at hand. ◆

THE HYPERLINKED LIFE

Live with Wisdom in an Age of Information Overload

THE FRAME

BY JUN YOUNG AND DAVID KINNAMAN

At a reunion with Jun's family members, everyone has traveled from far and wide for the purpose of reuniting. But while they are all — from the teens to the great aunts — enjoying the rare occasion of being in the same room, no one seems to be really present. Instead, everyone is fiddling with their gadgets.

Bathed in sunshine and sitting in paradise on a remote beach in Hawaii, David swings in a hammock, watching the kids play in the pool. His phone suddenly vibrates, urging him to address a crisis at work, and he spends the next hour fighting the fire with his thumbs. Mission accomplished — or was it?

A friend confides that he feels anxious whenever he's away from the Internet for too long. As a chaplain and trained counselor, this realization troubles him.

The *hyperlinked* life is here. It's familiar because we live it every day. Think about it. When was the last time you spent a whole day more than an arm's reach from your phone or computer? How often have you checked an app today to get some piece of information or to communicate with someone you have never actually met? What's your average response time when someone digitally summons you with a tweet, text, or tag? Have you been told by a friend, family member — or even your children — to "please put down your phone for just a minute"? Have easy access and email alerts made you more likely to work during vacation?

Enabled by mobile technology and fueled by countless apps and websites, the hyperlinked life feeds on digital information. Dr. Neil Postman, famed media critic and professor at NYU, reflects on the times:

> Information is now a commodity that can be bought and sold, or used as a form of entertainment, or worn like a garment to enhance one's status. It comes indiscriminately, directed at no one in particular, disconnected from usefulness; we are glutted with information, drowning in information, have no control over it, don't know what to do with it.[1]

What's fascinating about Postman's reflection is not how well it describes our current state but that he made this observation in 1990 — well before the popularization of the Internet, before smartphones or tablets, before Google and Facebook ever had domain names. Postman didn't know then that just two and a half decades later, the way we seek and find information would be fundamentally transformed and the glut of information would be exponential.

Today, smartphones are in the hands of 1.4 billion people,[2] and tablets, a more recent phenomenon, are outpacing smartphones in growth and adoption. Through computers and other gadgets, we are continuously plugged into a massive global information network comprised of websites, cloud services, complex databases, and other information systems. We use this network (the Net) to influence virtually every facet of life.

Fueling the Net is a socio-technical trend many refer to as *big data*.[3] Everything has gone digital, from music and videos to news and social media. We are generating exponentially more digital content than ever before. According to IBM, in 2012 people around the world created 2.5 quintillion (that's 1 followed by 18 zeros) bytes of data—every day![4] Information is being generated at such an incredible pace that 90% of all existing data on the planet was created in just the last two years.

Just as Postman posited, *we are glutted with information, drowning in information.* And for many of us, our response, it seems, is to jump right in.

Using our handy devices, we readily consume, interact with, and add to the Net. Around the world, in the next twenty-four hours, humans will text 188 billion times,[5] send 144 billion emails,[6] google 4.7 billion times,[7] download 30 million apps,[8] Skype for 2 billion minutes,[9] write 2.1 million blog posts,[10] and tweet 400 million times.[11]

Social critics have mixed views as to whether this digitally driven, information-saturated state is good or bad for society. Technophiles laud the benefits of digital—how it gives access of knowledge to more people in more places, connects us in new ways, and makes life easier in many respects, from banking to shopping to dating. On the other extreme are "Luddites," who fear that technology is degrading society, if not destroying it. And many of us are somewhere in the middle: unsure if technology is good or bad for us, but caught up in it all the same. Ample research supports both extremes, and while the debate is heated, most agree on one thing: The knowledge revolution is happening, and this way of life is here to stay.

The positive impact of a

HYPERLINKED LIFE

ALL ADULTS

1 / 56%
2 / 41%
3 / 32%
4 / 31%
5 / 29%

1 / *It's fun to learn new things*
2 / *I have greater confidence in my decisions*
3 / *I can keep others informed on important issues*
4 / *I can avoid bad decisions*
5 / *I feel like I have more control over my life*

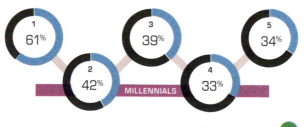

MILLENNIALS

1 / 61%
2 / 42%
3 / 39%
4 / 33%
5 / 34%

So, the concern, then, is how to live within it—and as Christians, how to live in it well. We believe that to do so will require *a theology of information.* What do we mean by that? We are referring to a deep and livable understanding of how God intends for humans to interact with the tools and information now so readily available.

Such a theology must start with an understanding of the technology, because while much can be said about the content that pulsates through this super network, it's not just the content that is shaping our lives; it is the medium itself.

As originally proposed by Marshal McLuhan and co-opted by countless media and cultural critics, *the medium is the message.* In other words, if you want to understand a given culture, pay attention to the methods and tools it uses to communicate. Today the prevalent tools for the expression and exchange of ideas are digital—the Internet, devices, apps—and they have opened the floodgates of information available to us.

Taken together, these modes of communication we have fashioned are now fashioning us. These technologies affect how we live, move, and have our being (see Acts 17:28). Here are three ways we see technology (the medium) changing the shape (the message) of our lives—and how a theology of information might address those changes.

We Are Self-Oriented: We no longer need to rely on major organizations and companies to develop ideas and products for us. We can create our own products, services, and experiences that conform to our own personal preferences. Current technology allows for greater transparency, which allows people to see the "inner workings" of a system and rewire it for themselves. A theology of information must prompt us to consider this question: How can we find wisdom from outside ourselves when digital tools keep putting the individual—me—at the center of the universe?

We Are Networked: We are seeing a growth of organic, symbiotic alliances, and the loss of traditional static structures. From business to religion to family and friends, relationships have become more dynamic, more transient, and more mutual. Just like the movie studios rely on a loose network of actors and crews, companies are starting to depend on consultants and freelancers instead of traditional employees. Friendships are developing along the same lines. As our families become more geographically diverse and defined less by genetics and more by mutual care and concern, we try to construct and reconstruct "families" wherever we need them. How do we apply the biblical ideal of community and inter-dependence in this age of digital networks?

We Are Collaborative: We often share information so effortlessly that our default behavior can be to work on something in a group rather than alone. Chances are the last time you decided to make a major purchase, you "collaborated" with a number of people who had already made that purchase: You read their reviews and trusted (or didn't trust) their ratings. What can we learn together about stewarding our collective influence and meaningfully impacting the lives of people around us?

Applying a Theology of Information

In many ways, we have become like the ancient civilization of Genesis 11, whose members said to each other, "Come, let us build ourselves a city, with a tower that reaches to the heavens, so that we may make a name for ourselves" (Genesis 11:4). As technology has become the idol of our time, we have begun to fashion our own digital "Tower of Babel."

As followers of Jesus, who have been warned against conforming to the pattern of this world (see Romans 12:2), we need to take time to evaluate this hyperlinked world, see it for what it is, and find ways to be transformed by the renewing of our minds in Christ. This is a theology of information and, to that end, we pose several questions:

- As a hyperlinked people, what kinds of relationships with technology and information are beneficial, ethical, godly?

- How does being hyperlinked affect our relationships, our minds, our souls?

- How can we avoid the cynicism of the transparent digital world in a way that enhances rather than tears down organizations and institutions (churches, colleges, governments, and businesses)?

- What will define wisdom in a digital world where an immense amount of knowledge can be accessed so quickly?

First, let's look at the shape of a hyperlinked life.

A Hyperlinked Life

The term *hyperlinked* seems appropriate to describe our super-networked, always-connected lives today. Here are three characteristics of a hyperlinked life:

Plugged-In and Always-On

With the proliferation of smart devices and ubiquitous access to the Internet, more people today are plugged-in at home, at work, and everywhere in between. Whether it's a smartphone in our pockets, a computer on our laps, a tablet in our hands, or a smart watch on our wrists, being online has never been easier. According to Barna's 2011 *Family and Technology Report*, many of us are spending more than eight hours a day plugged into the digital world.[12] And this not just a trend among the digitally savvy youth — it's a fact of twenty-first-century life for young and old. In fact, few (less than one out of ten) adults or youth say they take substantial breaks from technology.[13]

Our devices are wireless, yet we're more tethered than ever.

> *"When a text or message comes in, I usually stop what I'm doing to check it"*

42%

Millennials

36%

All adults

If the reality of a hyperlinked life is being plugged-in, then the expectation is to be always-on. Suddenly, we are perpetually reachable, ready to answer—and we expect the same of others. Email is the new snail mail, with texts, WhatsApp messages, tweets, and instant messaging enabling real-time, synchronous interactions. In a sense, we've found a way to be omnipresent.

Yet, this is where the convenience of instant communication often backfires. In this always-on etiquette, turning off or tuning out feels odd, even rude. In the not-too-distant past, beepers were reserved for doctors and firefighters who had to respond to crises at a moment's notice. Today we are all "on-call" for our friends, our colleagues, and others who want to reach us instantly. We are hyperlinked, our humanity underlined with that bright blue line, ready to be clicked and called to action at any time.

Data Dependent

We've all been there before. We're in the company of friends, family, or co-workers who are disputing a fact. Sides are taken, and both groups are sure they're right. Finally, someone whips out their phone to settle the draw.

We enjoy the luxury of information on demand, yet it reveals our dependency on data. This is another characteristic of a hyperlinked life.

According to Pew Research, smartphone users are part of "a new culture of real-time information seekers and problem solvers."[14] In the world of newspapers, radio, and television, we waited for information to come to us, typically at regularly scheduled times. These days, we constantly hunt and search for information through our mobile devices—anytime, anywhere. And because information on the Net is so easy to find, we've grown dependent on data to help manage our lives.

In the process of writing this book, both Jun and David took a count of how many times we checked our phones for information in one day. Try it sometime. Between email, texts, searches, news, RSS feeds, Facebook, weather, directions, calendar, shopping, music, and, occasionally, phone calls, we discovered we each reached for our phone more than one hundred times that day.

The vast amount of information and entertainment is just too enticing to ignore and too useful to live without.

Our data dependency is anything but unique. At the most recent All Things D conference, Internet analyst Mary Meeker reported that, on average, people use their mobile devices 150 times a day.[15] A global study by Cisco Systems reports that more than half of the 1,444 college students surveyed said the Internet and mobile devices are an integral part of daily life they can't live without.[16] If forced to choose, two-thirds of college students would choose an Internet connection instead of a car. We now have a term for the common fear of being disconnected from our gadgets: "nomophophia" (i.e., no-mobile-phone phobia). Another study by Cisco suggests that nine of ten people under the age of thirty suffer from nomophobia.[17]

As our devices become more sophisticated, they do more than just provide general information. Equipped with a variety of sensors, our gadgets know a lot about us — our location, habits, likes, and dislikes — and they provide us with useful information tailored to us personally. There's the scale that works wirelessly with your phone to not only track your weight and BMI but give you advice on how to eat better. It even sends you kudos for doing so. There's the watch that tells you how well you've been sleeping; it also vibrates to nudge you to get up and get active. As gadgets continue to become more useful — and they will — we will grow even more dependent on them and the data they provide.

In the hyperlinked life, if being plugged-in and

"*I get frustrated when I have conflicting pieces of information*"

60% All adults

67% Millennials

always-on gives us a sense of omnipresence, data dependency gives us a sense of omnipotence. More information gives us power to control the things in our lives that need to be managed. We rely on data to make decisions: small, insignificant ones (Is this restaurant worth going to? Will I need an umbrella tomorrow?) and big life-altering ones (Is this medical procedure safe? Should I marry him?). More information means less that is unknown, less doubt, and more confidence and control. As the Fitbit website says about its Wi-Fi smart scale, "When you're in control, stepping on the scale feels good."

Living with App-ification

Want to shop, travel, read, study, cook, grieve, or worship? There's an app for that! Apps have replaced the Web as our favorite way to access digital information.[18] More than 80% of the time spent on iOS and Android devices is spent inside apps versus the browser.[19] "Mobile app developers will 'appify' just about every interaction you can think of in your physical and digital worlds," says Scott Ellison of the research firm IDC.[20] Apps have become the language and common mode of interaction in a hyperlinked life.

Facebook's role in appifying relationships is perhaps the most profound and widespread example. In less than ten years, Facebook has amassed more than one billion users and reshaped the way we seek out and stay in touch with friends. We can compare friendship counts, befriend or unfriend, send love from afar, and stay updated on someone's life without ever having to actually talk to another person—all with the swipe of a finger on an app.

In many ways, appification simplifies life. And because we're busier than ever, simple is something we desperately seek. So we turn to apps as a way to make sense of life and manage it accordingly. Apps didn't exist six years ago, but today they are becoming not just our default way of interacting with the world but our primary way of thinking about the world.

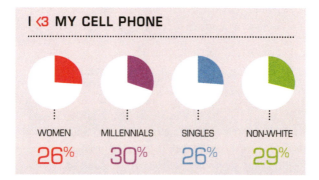

I <3 MY CELL PHONE

WOMEN	MILLENNIALS	SINGLES	NON-WHITE
26%	30%	26%	29%

Jun's seven-year-old daughter knew how to work apps before she knew how to read. And more than a few times she has tried to touch the television and other screens, thinking an app would appear. David's nine-year-old son asks for books to be "paused." Before he could read, he knew Google searches provided answers to perplexing questions. We are raising hyperlinked children who join us in the Information Age's "new normal" of being plugged-in and always-on, dependent on data, and seeing the world through apps.

The Hyperlinked Future

For those of us who have lived through the invention of the Internet and mobile computing, it feels like digital technology has finally reached a mature phase. But as most tech pundits will tell you, we've barely scratched the surface. Every day, tens of thousands of new apps are developed, and smarter, more powerful gadgets are designed to replace what's in our pockets and fill the gaps in our lives that have yet to be digitized. This modern digital world offers much to amuse, amaze, and delight us, enabling us to do things we didn't think possible just five years ago. For example, today we have the option of "hiring" an app as our personal assistant. It can send birthday greetings for us, nudge us when a friend posts troublesome news, and even remind us to dress appropriately tomorrow when it looks like it might rain.

During a recent airport layover, Jun enjoyed some good old-fashioned people watching, paying particular attention to interactions between people and their gadgets. Not surprisingly, every fourth or fifth person was staring, touching, or talking into some sort of digital screen. They were plugged-in, and most seemed engaged in some other world. Yet, something Jun hadn't noticed before hit home—how physically awkward and clunky these experiences really are. Plucking away at our phones with small screens. Gazing down while we're walking. Contorting our arms and posture over a laptop. Dangling headphone wires from our ears. Pushing past other travelers to a crowded recharging station. With all their dazzling, awe-inspiring qualities, our technologies have a long way to go before they play a seamless part in our daily activities.

Try this experiment at an airport, mall, or beach. Watch people's interactions with their digital devices. How people look while hovering over their Facebook accounts actually isn't their most flattering "face." And while you're at it, imagine with us the future of our hyperlinked society.

Imagining Our Digital Future

What will the world look like when the power of digital technologies becomes even more integrated into our homes, our vehicles, our workplaces, stores, and churches, and yes, our bodies?

Microsoft's Envisioning Center presents a compelling view of what the next stages of a hyperlinked lifestyle will look like. And how, in fact, it will change the way we live, work, and play in the near future.[21] Homes will have smart, digital, touch-screen surfaces everywhere—walls, counters, windows, appliances—that will always be listening, watching, anticipating needs, carrying out tasks, and providing the right information for every context. Workplaces will have the same qualities—every surface smart and touchable. There will no longer be a computer on every desktop because the *desktop* will be the computer, and it will be ready to do our bidding as it pays close attention to our movements, voice, facial expressions, and gaze.

But that's not all. We will rely on devices that are no longer in our pocket but physically attached to our bodies—even embedded inside. Always powered up and ready to go, this new generation of gadgets will be charged by light or perhaps the bioelectricity pulsating inside us. These

Watching out
FOR THE
WATCHERS

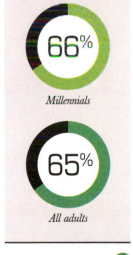

"I worry about how much information the government and businesses have about me"

66%

Millennials

65%

All adults

gadgets will take being hyperlinked to a whole new level. Without having to hold a phone or tablet, we will be plugged-in and fed all the information we need throughout the day. Directions to that new restaurant will be delivered straight into our digital visor (see Google's smart glasses project[22]). We will use the skin on our forearm to send a quick text (see Microsoft's "skinput" technology[23]). We will simply speak a message and it will be instantly routed to the person we intend to receive it. We will get real-time data on our vital signs, alerting us to potential threats to our health. People already make health decisions based on statistical predictions (see the aforementioned example of actress Angelina Jolie's preventive double mastectomy based on genetic information on page 23).

Imagine what other kinds of decisions we'll make with our bodies and our lives based on an even richer deliverable set of data. Fate and providence are replaced with data-driven choices as we veer toward the lives of cyborgs in the fantasy movies that both disturb and fascinate us.

Today, we already have close relationships with our devices. As artificial intelligence progresses, imagine how much more intimate these device-human relationships will become. Robots will be in our homes as servants and companions. Perhaps a virtual butler will greet us at the front door, already have dinner prepared, and ask about our day. Our children may be cared for and tutored by a virtual nanny. And perhaps our devices will become the objects of our affection and much more, as David Levy foresees in his book *Love and Sex with Robots*.[24]

Perhaps a few of these things seem far-off and others far-fetched. Wherever the road leads, it's likely that we who are living the hyperlinked life today are destined to lead the hyperlinked life of tomorrow. So it's important for us to consider what kind of relationships we currently have with technology and information and where all this might be going.

Truth and Consequences

The perks of the hyperlinked life are many, which is why so many of us gravitate toward this way of living. When we're plugged-in, we get instant access to anything we want to know and anyone we need to reach. With our devices in hand, we feel smarter, more equipped, more secure, more connected to a tapestry of communities and data sources.

Yet, the risk of the Information Age is that there's more information at our fingertips than we could ever consume. And shackled to the always-on expectations

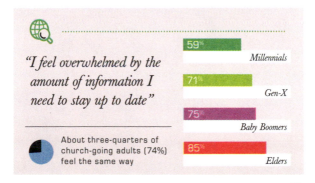

"I feel overwhelmed by the amount of information I need to stay up to date"

About three-quarters of church-going adults (74%) feel the same way

59% — Millennials
71% — Gen-X
75% — Baby Boomers
85% — Elders

of others can be overwhelming. In our FRAMES research, seven out of ten people surveyed agreed they feel overwhelmed by the amount of information they need to digest to stay up to date. Yet, most of us think we can fit more into our days than what is actually possible. Every minute is scheduled, and often even downtime is spent with eyes fixed on a screen. As we spend more of our waking hours hyperlinked, our ways of thinking and doing conform to this daily existence.

Here are a few questions to prove the point: Do your vacations seem more connected than ever, as though it's more difficult than ever to break away? Let's say you're out of cell phone range for a few hours. Do you find you're thinking about your email, Twitter, Instagram, Facebook, apps, or just plain old Internet service? Do you have a hard time sleeping if your cell phone isn't near you? Or if you travel to another country and literally have to "unplug" from your usual digital routines, don't you find it takes a few days to orient your habits around this new, less-hyperlinked life? And

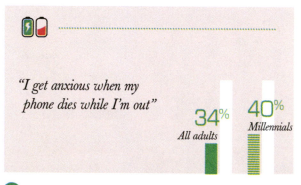

"I get anxious when my phone dies while I'm out"

34% *All adults*

40% *Millennials*

doesn't it feel good to be "back" home, back to your digital patterns and conveniences?

Many of us have drifted into these daily digital habits without much thought. After all, it's become the way of American life, and everyone we know lives it with us. But have we deeply considered the consequences of our digital dependence?

The Hyperlinked Brain

In his critically acclaimed book *The Shallows*, Nicholas Carr builds a strong case that the rise of the Internet as our primary information source has not only shaped our behaviors but already rewired the neural workings of our brains. The change is embedded deeply into how we think and so insidious that we may not even be aware our minds are being altered.

> It's not just that we tend to use the Net regularly, even obsessively. It's that the Net delivers precisely the kind of sensory and cognitive stimuli — repetitive, intensive, interactive, addictive — that have been shown to result in strong and rapid alterations in brain circuits and functions. With the exception of alphabet and number systems, the Net may well be the single most powerful mind-altering technology that has ever come into general use.[25]

Carr argues that, as people interact with the frenetic, fast-paced, parceled approach of digital media, the ability to practice deep and creative thought for sustained periods of time diminishes. In other words, being hyperlinked is dumbing us down. It may be a controversial argument, but it's far from new. In the mid-1980s, Neil Postman came to a similar conclusion about television in his popular book *Amusing Ourselves to Death*.[26]

Beyond our abilities to learn and consume knowledge, the hyperlinked lifestyle affects other functions of the brain. Digital experiences — from the thrills of online gaming to the sense of accomplishment when we get lots of "likes" on Facebook — stimulate the "pleasure center" in our brains, which can lead to psychological consequences, from mindless habits to severe addictions. The government of South Korea, the most connected country on the planet where 8% of people under the age of thirty-nine are addicted to the Internet, has instituted a gaming curfew to help curtail gaming addictions that have led to instances of exhaustion, malnutrition, and death.[27]

Being hyperlinked has also affected the brain's abilities to rest. Psychologists Dr. Archibald Hart and Dr. Sylvia Hart Frejd explain that constant excitement or demands from technology gadgets can cause our brains to produce excessive amounts of cortisol.[28] Typically, cortisol is good for us because it helps us deal with stressful situations, but prolonged elevated levels of cortisol can lead to serious psychological changes, such as anxiety disorders. If we fill our hours with ongoing media-rich connectedness, we deny ourselves a different kind of richness that silence, solitude, and contemplation can offer. And over time, this degrades our brain's ability to be at peace.

Skimming through Life

As a result, the hyperlinked brain skims through life. How else can we cope when we're at once overwhelmed by and over-dependent on the richness of the Net? For those of you who went to college or graduate school, think back to being assigned way too much reading than could possibly fit into the quarter. The only way to survive was to skim through the materials and glean as much knowledge as possible. For the most part, this can work. But undoubtedly, there were important truths missed, nuances overlooked, valuable insights passed by in a rush. Today, life seems like a never-ending college course of unrealistic expectations — admittedly, many of which are self-imposed. Rather than unplugging from the Net, our brains are conditioned to skim the surface of our daily activities — in-boxes, news feeds, Web pages, infographics, blogs, tweets — seldom going deeply.

But what important things are we missing in the skimming? We agree with George Bernard Shaw that

Adults surveyed said:

54% *"There are times when I think I actually have too much information"*

This isn't just the fuddy-duddies either. More than half of Millennials (56%) feel the same.

the biggest flaw of communication is the assumption that it has happened. Skimming has become a frequent thing for most us these days and maybe for you too. Both David and Jun can recount recent times of being caught flatfooted, having forgotten or missed an important piece of information in an email or text we thought we had read fully. Even when we concentrate on reading more carefully instead of just skimming, the eyes get impatient and the fingers start scrolling. Both of us admit it has become harder to read books from start to finish and more difficult to sink deeply into long conversations.

The problem here is not that we're prone to skim through life (after all, it's likely that in this age of information overload, most of the banal data we receive during the day only deserves a quick scan). The issue is that our brains are changing. And our ability to concentrate, to rest, and to think deeply is waning in the process. In fact, it's possible that we might never be able to reverse the effects of the hyperlinked brain.

Hyperlinked Relationships

A relationship between two people can be described as a long, sustained conversation. Think about your closest friend or family member. The story of that relationship has been formed and sustained through dialogue. The deep talks, the fights, the jokes, the sorrow and joy, and the meaningful and meaningless are all shared through the script of your ongoing conversations. When the talking stops, the friendship dies.

The hyperlinked life is changing this dynamic and redefining friendship.

Relationships mediated by technology are not new, of course. Since the invention of the telegraph, telephone, email, and video conferencing, people have found ways to connect through devices. What makes hyperlinked relationships different is that they are nurtured primarily, if not solely, through social media. Facebook, of course, comes to mind immediately with more than 15% of the world population using it to build hyperlinked friendships. But "friendship," as it's used here, is something different than the traditional definition. Any one of us who has hundreds if not thousands of "Facebook friends" knows that dynamic is definitively different than having a personal friendship with someone.

In social media like Facebook, the concept of friendship is culturally recoded. If we want to be someone's friend, we simply send a request. If that person hits accept, we're friends! And our interactions online are composed of a series of digital expressions — "likes," "comments," "posts," and perhaps the occasional "chat," most of which aren't targeted solely toward us. Such a friendship doesn't demand much from us. And if the talking stops, the friendship remains intact. Many of these friendships were formed by traditional means (school friends, previous colleagues, friends who have moved away), though it has become increasingly common to build new friends exclusively online. For example, online virtual worlds like Second Life, which has twenty million "residents," give people a chance to create a second self, complete with friends, spouses, and children "played" by other users. A new app called Highlight bypasses the request/accept step of typical social media apps and surfaces information about the people about one hundred yards around you, whether or not they are "friends." If someone interesting crosses your path, Highlight will tell you more about them.[29]

There's natural appeal to hyperlinked relationships. They take just a few clicks to initiate, and we can connect with people around the world regardless of location or time zone. Facebook, for example, allowed Jun to reconnect with his cousins in the Philippines, whom he hadn't seen for twenty years. Once connected, it feels like any one of these friends is just a click away. Maintaining hundreds, if not thousands, of online friendships requires much less investment of our time and attention than off-line friendships. Off-line friendships require spending time together — over coffee, on the phone, during the weekends. Off-line friendships require attention and effort, plus they're messy because people's lives are messy.

In contrast, hyperlinked friendships are much more compatible to this age of information overload. We can maintain hyperlinked relationships by digitizing them and managing them through devices and apps. We "keep up" by scrolling through status messages. We've replaced one-to-one communication with one-to-many communication. We broadcast our lives before a digital network, where some people tune in and others don't.

Of course, social media can also help nurture and improve our off-line relationships. This is true for both

David and Jun: By using texts, we stay in constant contact throughout the day with our spouses. Both of our companies have employees working from different locations, but we get things done throughout the day via instant messaging, email, texts, and Skype. The power of digital tools has enhanced many of our client interactions and friendships.

Trouble with hyperlinked relationships appears when they become our primary source for companionship. There's a propensity to reduce people to just one of the many data sources transmitting information. We "skim" these friendships just like we do with every other piece of information that calls for our attention. Friendships become just another node in the digital life we have to manage, just another app among the dozens on our screens that we can "play" when we have a moment and that we can turn off when it's inconvenient. Some research has found that deep, healthy friendships can form and be sustained online. Other studies conclude a life made up of mostly hyperlinked relationships generates multitudes of connections, but few bonds. If we focus exclusively on our online relationships, we opt for the illusion of companionship without the requirements and blessings of real friendship.

A Toll on Off-Line Relationships

While the vehement debate on whether or not hyperlinked friendships are "real" continues, we have to consider another reality. Our always-on lifestyle has taken a toll on our off-line relationships. In her book *Alone Together*, MIT professor and clinical psychotherapist Sherry Turkle describes our deepening relationship with technologies.[30] She laments that many of us have arrived at the point where we've come to expect more from technology than we do from each other. We have an intimate relationship with our gadgets and the online world that fuels them. They are always with us, serving as reliable assistants, trusted advisers, close companions. There is a growing population of people who require hourly dosages of texting, emails, Facebook, and the like to feel connected to friends, family, and colleagues. The irony is that when we plug in to the Net, we unplug from the room we're in and the people there who seek our attention.

A few weeks ago, Jun was at the park with his kids. Waiting to be found during a game of hide-and-seek, he pulled out his phone. Then an eerie moment occurred when he looked around and realized every parent at the park was tinkering with a phone. Jun sheepishly put his away.

David recalls his daughter's recent imperative: "Dad, put Twitter away so you can help me with my homework!"

Throughout the day, while we're in conversations, reading a book, watching TV, working, or driving, we allow ourselves to be interrupted by digital tidbits blinking on our phone or the sudden urge to post what we're doing right now. We not only allow distractions, we crave them. We thrive on distractions. It's not a big mental leap to realize there's something inherently odd about this, but we go on because our commitment to our crowd of "friends" and "followers" compels us to remain up to date.

Relying primarily on hyperlinked relationships, which are sustained by short bursts of witty expressions, the danger is that our ability to handle the give and take of real conversations will atrophy. Will we forget the power of eye contact and the warm touch of a friend who really cares? As we skim relationships, will we lose the ability to read nonverbal signals, to hear in someone's voice that everything isn't, in reality, okay?

Maybe. But what's most disturbing about investing wholly in hyperlinked relationships isn't that we can't apply the social skills required to nurture off-line friendships. It's that we won't want to. They will simply require too much work for a payoff that takes too long.

"I think my personal electronics sometimes separate me from other people"

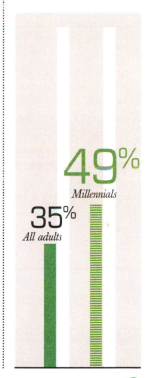

49%
Millennials

35%
All adults

Hyperlinked Work

A few years ago, Jun's colleague and friend Paul said something about his work that has stuck with us ever since: "I find that my job these days is really not much more than pixel-pushing," Paul said. "Most of the day, I'm staring at my computer and moving pixels around. I click here and something happens. I double click there and some other thing gets done. I barely talk to anyone, at least not in person. I manipulate little dots on a screen and get paid lots for it!"

Many jobs today, especially in corporate America, can be described as pixel-pushing. "Information workers" manipulate little dots on a screen to analyze, create, express, and make meaning of information. Sometimes the pixels are email, other times documents or applications. And because these tasks can be accomplished using connected devices, our jobs demand that we be hyperlinked. That is, we are expected to be plugged-in and always-on, and we are deluged with more information than we can possibly process during a reasonable workday.

A growing multitude of workers in today's workforce are now classified as "mobile workers." The office is no longer bound to a building and a cubicle. With the right mobile devices, people can work from anywhere — their living room, at a coffee shop, on a plane, or even from a hammock in Hawaii. The expectation, of course, is that if we are able to work anywhere, we should be *willing* to work anywhere — and all the time. Plugged-in and always-on, this work style is relentless.

One late afternoon, one of Jun's clients sent an urgent instant message, panicked that he couldn't reach one of Jun's colleagues.

"Where is she?" he demanded. "Can you find her and tell her to contact me right away?" A few minutes later, Jun was able to reach the colleague and discovered she had just finished a phone call with this exact client and had left her desk for a few minutes for a restroom break. When Jun explained the situation to the client, his response was, "I need you guys to be reachable anytime during the day, no matter what!"

At the time his expectation seemed outrageous. But it represents the logical progression of hyperlinked work. We're always-on, ready to serve—just like all those gadgets. We've freed ourselves from the confining walls of the office only to find we've accepted

All day long

I CHECK MY PHONE...

40% *All adults*   **56**% *Millennials*

First thing in the morning

33% *All adults*   **54**% *Millennials*

Right before bed

6% *All adults*   **12**% *Millennials*

In the middle of the night

a more severe trap. Hyperlinked to our work, we are rarely out of reach from the continuously imminent crisis that calls out for our help. The good news is that our devices and apps make it fairly easy to respond. The bad news is that we are expected to respond—no matter what—at home during dinner, at the park with our kids, at a concert with friends, and on vacation in a far-off place.

If your job has become mostly about writing and responding to email, texts, or another form of pixel-pushing, you are part of the hyperlinked work style. Whatever the job title, for many of us the measure of success is our ability to manage and manipulate information—and lots of it.

Susan, a senior manager who leads a group of thirty people in a high-tech firm, laments, "I get around six hundred emails every day. I'm in meetings most of the day, so it's mathematically impossible to respond to all of them even though I work every evening after I put the kids to bed and on most weekends. So I triage my in-box and reply to the most urgent issues and also emails that come from my superiors. The rest I just ignore. I figure if they really want a response, they'll send me a reminder." And yet, Susan has received feedback from colleagues that she isn't responsive enough and that as a leader, she seems distant and uncaring. This has been Susan's daily reality for more than five years. She's exhausted, but she loves the work and is seen by her company as an outstanding performer because she is able to handle so much. She recently received a promotion, so her team will now double in size.

For Susan and for many of us, information overload at work has reached an all-time high. A decade ago, people called it "drinking from a fire hose." Today, it's more like drinking from Niagara Falls. Big data feeds this deluge, and our devices serve it up for constant consumption. There are too many tasks, too many projects, too many documents to sift through, too many people to please. So today's workers multitask and triage as best they can, hoping that at some point the flow will let up. Both Jun and David interact with clients from different companies and various departments, and we have seen this frenetic, overwhelming pace across a variety of workplaces. We have witnessed this hyperlinked work life lead to eroded marriages, poor health, and a joyless existence.

Hyperlinked Faith

Two foundational questions that shape our faith and our lives are at the core of spiritual formation: Who is God? and Who am I? For better or worse, our way of life today—the hyperlinked lifestyle—impacts the answers to these questions.

As we can see in the FRAMES research, Christians, as much as anyone else, are living the hyperlinked life. As part of this study, we interviewed a sample of U.S. adults and analyzed the findings into four groups: practicing Christians under forty, practicing Christians forty or over, non-practicing Christians, and non-Christians. In general, the responses to questions about the hyperlinked life were consistent across the four groups. Practicing Christians were the group that most strongly agreed they felt "overwhelmed by the amount of information they need to digest to stay up to date." When it comes to Internet dependency, Christians and non-Christians alike reported they "would struggle to go more than one day without Internet access." Among the groups surveyed, those under forty (whether Christian or not) were most likely to agree with this statement (47% of Millennials, 56% of Gen-Xers).

The general findings of our study suggest that Christians grapple with the hyperlinked lifestyle, certainly as much as non-Christians and perhaps, in some cases, more so than non-Christians. This shouldn't be surprising because the practices of a hyperlinked life are reshaping the spiritual disciplines of Christian faith. A friend shares his concern: "I'm having a hard time doing morning devotions. My first inclination is to reach for my phone and see what's happening. At church, during the sermon, I use my phone to look up Scripture, but then I end up checking email, sports, news, and all that."

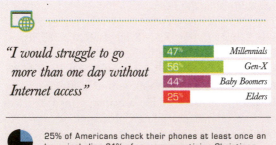

"I would struggle to go more than one day without Internet access"

47%	Millennials
56%	Gen-X
44%	Baby Boomers
25%	Elders

25% of Americans check their phones at least once an hour, including 31% of younger practicing Christians

An hour of meditative prayer and solitude seems out of touch in a hectic, always-on, 140-characters-or-less world. Apps like Seven:Fourteen and countless others are appifying prayer, intending to make prayer easier and more fun by sending participants reminders, short devotionals, a place to post prayers—even an interactive map that shows who else is praying. Church leaders are not only tolerating phone usage during sermons, many now encourage it, hoping a tweet or post will draw others to faith and/or church.

The hyperlinked life offers some advantages to the development of our faith. We have instant access to troves of information that can help nurture our faith—devotionals, sermon notes, biblical translations and expositions, podcasts, worship music, and so on. On the Net, there is always someone available to pray with us.[31] Online resources have also made it easier for people struggling in situations around the world where living out a Christian faith may have hostile consequences.

But we also have to consider how the frenzy of this information-drenched lifestyle aligns with God's vision for our lives. How well does the hyperlinked life live up to the promise Jesus made in John 10:10—"I have come that they may have life, and have it to the full"? We certainly have a life full of information, but our daily lives, our relationships, and our time to think and be all seem to be depleted.

In this age of information overload, we need to consider a theology of information. Mentioned earlier, information technology has become the idol of our slice of history. In pursuit of the powers technology promises, with the same hubris that possessed our ancestors, we have created a digital "Tower of Babel" reaching to the clouds. This time, the tower is not a rising city made of stone and mortar, but a vast digital network that's bigger than anything we can imagine, stores all of human knowledge, and is impossible to shut down. Of course, as history proves, the world is quite good at fashioning new idols for us to worship. The Net is just the latest. We don't know if the Internet is the "greatest threat" to Christianity as some have proposed, but we do think it's the most profound catalyst in our culture today, shaping how we live, work, learn, love, and worship. As with any idol we've created and put in a high place in our lives, the risk, as Scripture warns us, is not just that these idols become the objects of our worship but also our identity.

> But their idols are silver and gold, made by human hands. They have mouths, but cannot speak, eyes, but cannot see. They have ears, but cannot hear, noses, but cannot smell. They have hands, but cannot feel, feet, but cannot walk, nor can they utter a sound with their throats. Those who make them will be like them, and so will all who trust in them. (Ps. 115:4–8)

Wisdom for the Digital Age

So what are we to do with the reality of hyperlinked lives? Perhaps the most important thing we can do in response to the knowledge revolution is to learn and practice the timeless art of wisdom—wise living for the digital age. Ironically, we live in the most information-rich period in history, yet how many of us feel we are living with more wisdom? With more discernment? With deeper friendships or ample time? We live like virtual kings and queens when it comes to the access to and sheer amount of data we have about ourselves and our world. But being glutted with insta-knowledge hasn't always made our lives better.

For our purposes, let's define wisdom as "being smart about how to have a meaningful life while being humble enough to admit we have a lot to learn." Whether you are a Christian or come from another faith perspective, you as well as everyone else could benefit by finding this kind of wisdom.

We find lots of inspiration and instruction on the way of wisdom in Scripture. As Proverbs 9:10 says, "The fear of the LORD is the beginning of wisdom." This reminds us that wisdom is elusive and hard to find. Being informed is the easy road; living with wisdom is the more difficult journey. As the New Testament writer Paul says, "Do not conform to the pattern of this world, but be transformed by the renewing of your mind" (Romans 12:2). We would argue that it is more difficult than ever for believers to put this admonition into practice during the era of hyperlinked lives. But it can be done and ought to be our goal today, as it has been for centuries of Christians.

The rest of this FRAME, then, will address ways to add more wisdom to our digital diet — seven ideas and practices that will help us live more meaningfully and more humbly.

1. *Get the big picture of the digital knowledge revolution.*

We believe that most people have wrong or incomplete ideas about the digital revolution. We need the right perspective on the knowledge revolution to view it how God would have us do so. Much of this FRAME, in fact, is intended to point out the remarkable privilege of being alive at this time in history.

David's book *You Lost Me* developed the idea of the pivotal point the digital culture represents. He makes the argument that revolutions in information technology also affect how we relate to institutions, like the church. And this has been true throughout history. Think of Martin Luther when he nailed his ninety-five theses to that door in Wittenberg, Germany, nearly five hundred years ago. Little did he realize how the power of the printing press would popularize his writing, allowing him to impact thousands more than mere scribes could have ever reached. He was so struck by the power of the knowledge revolution of his day that he described the technical process of *printing* as "God's highest and extremist act of grace, whereby the business of the Gospel is driven forward." What a remarkable, prescient, and *wise* point of view on his times.

What can we learn from this? Some critics are quite dismissive of the effects of the digital world. They reason there is nothing new and that humans are still basically the same creatures with or without iPhones. Fair enough. But ignoring the large sweep of our cultural and digital moment feels like poor stewardship and a failure of imagination.

Others realize large social changes are afoot but claim the digital revolution is akin to massive addiction of the populace. Since our patterns of behavior with digital devices and screens parallel those of addictive behaviors, these critics say we should treat media and technology like the addictive tools they have become. However, we believe addiction is a limiting metaphor. Psychotherapist Sherry Turkle argues, "To combat addiction, you have to discard the addicting substance. But we are not going to 'get rid' of the Internet."[32] Nor are we unplugging completely. We are too far in, and the knowledge revolution is too good. But this overwhelming pace, with its consequences for our lives, is unacceptable. How, then, shall we live?

The answer is not as simple as decreasing our on-screen time (though that can be part of the solution for many of us). We have to become more aware of our *calling* as a hyperlinked people: what we are called to do and who we are called to be when we are plugged-in. Yes, we have become bionic—fully human but with some of our natural faculties enhanced by technology. But our God has not changed. He is "the same yesterday and today and forever" (Hebrews 13:8). And he still "works for the good of those who love him, who have been called according to his purpose" (Romans 8:28).

Some of us need to be reminded that technology is not something to fear, hate, or reject. Maybe you are on the side of the equation that wishes the digital revolution had waited until you were long gone, someone who might never say you love your cell phone. But it is helpful to remember this: We have all benefitted in some way from the digitization of knowledge; it is a wonderful privilege. And we should all, in some way, practice gratefulness to God because we are alive during this historic period of human history.

Others have to be reminded that technology should not define our lives nor be the center of them. We must put technology in its rightful position — not as an idol, but as one of the tools we use to get things done. Technology is part of the way of wisdom: something that makes us smarter about meaningful living and more humble about all we don't really understand. As Christians, like Luther, we should come to realize today's technology can be a domain of God's grace and a way for the gospel to go forward. For the Christ-follower, therefore, wisdom in the hyperlinked era isn't just about fulfilling our own desires for our own purposes, but those of Jesus.

2. Find your own place in this revolution, your own unique relationship to technology.

We ought to consider becoming more aware of our digital selves. When it comes to human behavior, the road to change begins with Spirit-driven understanding. The deeper we survey the landscape of our actions, the better map we have for navigating and even redirecting the paths of our habits. Each of us has a relationship with the gadgets in our lives and all the information they provide. Let's take time to understand that relationship for what it is.

One of the most direct ways to do this is to go on a

digital detox. Try this: Spend a full day, perhaps even a weekend, completely unplugged from your favorite gadgets. We think you'll begin to realize your reliance on digital screens and how that may be affecting the way you live your life. If you are like us, you will likely reach for your device to post a thought or text a friend or look something up and find you'll need to hold your thoughts to yourself, talk to someone close by, or be patient and wait for that piece of information to come some other time.

During your detox, pay attention to your reactions and feelings. How hard is this for you? Are you feeling anxious, disempowered, or simply relieved?

You can also become more aware of your relationship with technology by keeping a technology-use journal for a week. Basically, pay attention to your technology use and jot down when, how, and how long you're using your gadgets throughout the day (e.g., 8:00 a.m., Checked phone for weather and email, 7 minutes). To some of you, this will seem like overly detailed busywork. But the reward is at the end of the week when you'll have a much better understanding of how you spend your time online. Then the hard work begins, because knowing the reality of your relationship with technology, you'll be faced with some important questions: Is this how I should be spending my days? How hooked am I on gadgets and information? Is my relationship with my favorite devices more of a help or hindrance to my purpose in life? How are my habits shaping who I am, and is that who I want to be?

3. Practice digital Sabbath.

We have already talked about a digital detox, which can happen once or twice throughout the year. But perhaps the most important way to put your dependence on technology in balance is to go on a weekly digital Sabbath. This is the ancient concept—one of the Ten Commandments we often ignore—of taking one day a week to rest (see Exodus 20:8–10). In our research, we have learned that fewer than one in ten Christian families take anything like a digital Sabbath. And, as we have noted, many of us don't have proper boundaries with technology during the week because we sleep with and wake up next to our smartphones. So shoot for a full day a week when you turn off all your digital devices (or at least reserve them for true communication like phone calls and Skype chats with distant family and friends). Give yourself a true break from the screens in your life.

We can also apply the Sabbath concept to everyday life, generally trying to spend less time online *each day*. We like to call it "going analog." Replace screen time with more face time. Take long walks. Invite a friend to have coffee with you. Watch more sunsets. Write a letter. Make something by hand. Look a loved one deeply in his or her eyes. Basically, think about all the things you do on restful vacations and practice these during the week.

Digital Sabbath practices for you may be more about reshaping your everyday technology habits—the ones that lead to feelings of being overwhelmed, distracted, and fragmented. Such practices might include intentionally planning what three hours a day you'll respond to email, the rest of the time minimizing your email screen and turning off the alert badge. Using your phone only for communication during your work day (no Twitter or sports scores or Instagram). Setting your phone in a basket by your front door when you walk in at night and leaving it there until bedtime. Or designating a "no phone" room in your house, where everyone can regularly gather for a few hours a day. (See the Re/Frame on page 79, written by twentysomething Brandon Schulz about what his digital Sabbath practice has taught him.)

By the way, maybe your job requires a lot of pixel-pushing like we described earlier. If so, you might be thinking that it would be even harder for you to practice these disciplines or to ever truly "go analog." Well, it may be true that your *livelihood* is deeply embedded in your productivity while pushing pixels. Good for you; you have arrived as a knowledge worker in a knowledge economy. But here is the caveat: We think your *well-being* is all the more connected to being able to stay off the grid at regular and healthy intervals.

Think of it like a weekly (or in some way routine) digital diet, and try it for yourself. It will be hard at first, but you'll probably get more done, have better conversations, sleep more soundly, and focus on what is at hand, unleashing your ability to "work at [whatever you do] with all your heart, as working for the Lord" (Colossians 3:23), rather than getting sidetracked by a stream of digital interruptions. Such Sabbath practices will require self-discipline and setting boundaries with work and other responsibilities. But we think creating

#BarnaFrames

more analog moments in our hyperlinked lives will help rest and renew our minds, sharpen our people skills, and give us more space for the "fullness" Jesus describes.

4. Develop hyperlinked habits that define the real you, and the you that you want to be.

A fourth response we should have to the hyperlinked era is to be intentional about the kinds of people we want to be online. One way of putting this is that we need to be sure we don't cultivate two different versions of ourselves: our online self versus our off-line self. Are we Instagramming a perfect life? Are we presenting a fair picture of ourselves online? Are we "posing" for the digital camera more than we should?

Jocelyn, a forty-two-year-old receptionist, posts multiple times a day on Facebook but admits she is not presenting her true self online. Her profile and posts are tempered and much more positive than how she actually thinks. Apparently, she is "friends" with her manager at work, so she is careful to project an image that her employer would deem appropriate.

Of course, we have to be careful not to expose too much of ourselves online — there is wisdom in restraint. But there are also dangers inherent in cultivating two different lives. A carefully composed digital persona often leaves little room for true vulnerability, real-life struggles, or even the mundane (but often spiritually rich) tasks and habits of daily life. So how can we be intentional about living an honest and edifying digital life? Here are a few suggestions:

- In your digital life, focus on cultivating a specific spiritual "fruit" each week—love, joy, peace, patience (forbearance), kindness, goodness, faithfulness, gentleness, or self-control (see Galatians 5:22–23). More to the point, would our friends, clients, and critics say these godly characteristics define our digital profile?

- Allow your distinctive spiritual profile—the unique calling and gifts God has given you—to shine through your digital footprint. Maybe you are a fantastic encourager. Or a person who loves to pray for others. Or that person who is able to say tough things in a way that is gracious and grace-filled. How can technology enhance your "spiritual DNA" by revealing more of what God has made you to be?

- Take pride in being countercultural. It's easy to do things online that you see others doing: putting out the humble brag on Twitter, passing along gossip on Facebook, posing for the digital camera on Instagram, or being just plain mean about politicians or leaders with whom you disagree. In what way do you exhibit habits that are different from the digital herd?

- This idea of multiple digital personalities is something we have to pay particular attention to among teens and young adults, who are innately comfortable with their digital devices but who often struggle to learn how to be fully themselves in both digital and analog roles. How can we best be fully ourselves online and offline?

Which brings us to our fifth suggestion.

5. Mentor (and be mentored by) the next generation.

The youngest generations have the most to gain and the most to lose as the hyperlinked era comes of age. They also have more to give because they are true digital natives—they haven't witnessed the evolution of the Information Age; they were simply born into it. So what does this mean for us? As Christian communities, we need to work hard to mentor and develop the next generation of Christ-followers. While it's here to stay, this hyperlinked world is still news, so there's still a chance for us to make course corrections.

The best course correction we can make is to raise our children and grandchildren to be true biblical stewards of this new knowledge revolution. We can help them step back and realize the implications of a hyperlinked life—both the realities of *what is* and the potential of *what should be*. We need to understand the context for the rewards and risks we face when technology becomes so intertwined with how we build relationships, get stuff done, and live out our faith. We need to open up the possibility that we can (and should) shift aspects of our relationship with technology—that we don't have to accept things as they are, but indeed, have the power to make changes. We can warn those younger than we are that technology will become an idol if we let it.

But we also need to be humble enough to listen to the next generation and realize staying up to date with new technology does have real advantages. Emerging leaders partnering with established leaders—mentoring and reverse mentoring—to develop perspectives and solutions to handling the hyperlinked life.

Imagine what life will be like for future generations. If we stay on our current path, our great-grandchildren will know less and less of the unquantifiable power of long conversations, eye contact, and moments of togetherness and shared silence. So we need to teach children how to do these things well. Of course, we have to start by doing them well ourselves. We can do our best to help prepare the next generation for today's world, but we'll have to accept that all we can do is nurture in them the wisdom to face a future we can't possibly imagine.

6. Redefine stewardship to include technology.

This suggestion is based on our belief that one of the most important aspects of hyperlinked living is to enlarge our definition of stewardship—from time, treasure, and talent to also include technology. There is little doubt that today's digital world is driving how we spend our time, how we use our money, and what we make (or don't make) of our talents.

- **Time**—How does the digital world make demands of your time that are realistic or unrealistic?

- **Treasure**—How is your use of technology affecting your financial resources? Are you spending your valuable cash on things that are important to what God wants you to do?

- **Talent**—Are you using technology to become the best version of the person God wants you to be? Is the knowledge revolution helping to create in you a person who is more capably serving God?

Another aspect of stewardship is recognizing the significance of people who work in information industries and technology industries. This includes print and broadcast journalism; arts, entertainment, and media; computer and software companies; writing, research, and analysis; and many more sectors of today's society. Everything we watch, read, or hear is a form of digitized information. A video game is a type of information content. Music and movies are too. What Peter Drucker called the "knowledge economy"[33] has come of age. In this respect, we need to prepare a generation of knowledge workers for lives of purpose in these and many related fields—and empower those who are already serving in them with a sense of the weight and impact of their vocation.

Speaking now to pastors, the idea of stewarding the hyperlinked world means providing God's people with a broader set of ideas about stewardship. How can you help people make sense of the information barrage? How can they keep from putting themselves at the center of the digital universe when everything about our devices makes us more narcissistic? What does a theology of information look like for the people in your church? How can you articulate the needed shift from using people and loving our devices to loving people and using our devices?

7. *Be more discerning about whom and what to trust.*

Finally, if we are living in an era of information overload, we need better filters for deciding what sources we can trust and "facts" we can believe.

One of the challenges Christians face is finding credible information about our world that comes from a rich theological point of view. Naturally, this is where the role of the Bible comes in; we believe it is the most reliable source of wisdom about life because it represents God's Word to his people. In an era when the line between fact and error, truth and falsehood, certainty and feeling is blurry, Scripture provides a light into dark places. So, clearly, we believe hyperlinked Christians need to be people of the Book.

But beyond that, how can we discern between good and bad information—for instance, when we do what hyperlinked people do and follow a link to an article or study or blog? Here are five key questions to ask about any information:

1 Who or what organization is producing this information?

2 What might be their reason for doing so?

3 Do I believe or distrust this information simply because it confirms my preexisting viewpoint on the subject? Or am I willing to be open-minded and even swayed—within the boundaries of biblical truth?

BELIEVING WHAT WE READ

*What criteria do you use to know the
information you find online is true?*

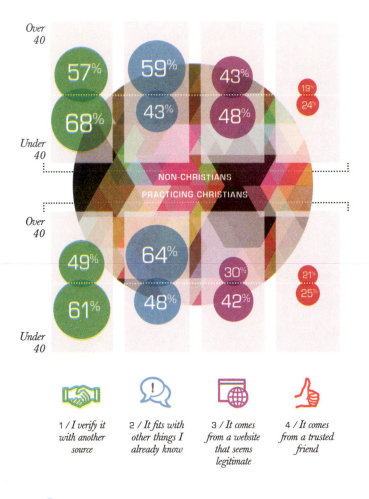

Over 40
57%   59%   43%   19%

Under 40
68%   43%   48%   24%

NON-CHRISTIANS

PRACTICING CHRISTIANS

Over 40
49%   64%   30%   21%

Under 40
61%   48%   42%   25%

1 / I verify it
with another
source

2 / It fits with
other things I
already know

3 / It comes
from a website
that seems
legitimate

4 / It comes
from a trusted
friend

4 Does this information help me live a more meaningful, God-honoring, and humble life?

5 What is this information asking me to love? Is this asking me, as a Christian, to love the things Jesus loves? Or is it making me more fearful and frustrated by making me believe the worst about people or the world?

Now, more than ever, everyone wants a piece of your mind. The question is this: Who will you allow to influence the way you think and act? As we said at the outset of this FRAME, we are all bombarded with information. How will you turn this barrage into a life of greater meaning and purpose?

A Final Word

We set out in this FRAME to describe the wonders and pitfalls of our digital domain. Hopefully, you've gained some new insights and perspectives about the knowledge revolution and how it has created hyperlinked lives.

Our culture is more complex, in large part due to the technologies of the world we inhabit. Ironically, life seems harder for many of us, not easier. But maybe all we really need is to relearn wisdom.

Of course, wisdom will always be more than a click away.

THE HYPERLINKED LIFE

Live with Wisdom in an Age of Information Overload

RE/FRAME

BY BRANDON SCHULZ

I am living the hyperlinked life.

I'm in my twenties. I can't really remember a time before the Internet. I don't have the faintest idea how to use a physical map. An actual phone conversation is cumbersome. Email feels slow, and I connect with friends every day in at least five different digital spaces.

I am living the hyperlinked life. But I am not hyperlinked.

I haven't always been able to say that. A few years ago, I realized I wasn't living the way I wanted to. I was immersed in a digital existence, online practically 24/7 and never without ten tabs open at a time, plus my phone at my side and an IM window always open. I was distracted, displaced, and feeling the effects. It's all too easy to blame our cultural vices on technology. But here's the truth: Technology doesn't pollute your character, it reveals it.

To see what I mean, try this simple test: First, put away, shut down, or unplug all your media devices. See how long you can last without them, and in the meantime, pay attention to what you think and feel. Then ask yourself this question: Do I use technology in a way that empowers me to love God, my community, and myself?

The only person responsible for the answer to this question is you. And when I finally began to understand that for myself, I started to take stock of the way I was living and determined to make some changes.

So let's look more closely at the character our hyperlinked lives are revealing, and how we might make practical changes as a result. These are four of the personal changes I've made in my own life.

Make a Short Stack

When my friends and I go out to dinner, we often stack our phones in the middle of the table. And we all agree that no matter how many ringtones, vibrations, or digital sound-offs are made, we won't touch our phones for the entire meal. And if someone does reach for their phone? They have to buy everyone dinner. Trust me— no one ever does.

Instead, we talk to each other, look one another in the eye, and experience the richness of being fully present. It is in these interactions that I find the community so many of my generation desperately desires. After discovering this simple trick of "the short stack," I began to crave its benefits. The imitation of intimacy found through my phone was no match for the real thing I could find by engaging with people physically around me. Soon enough, this became my personal standard, and I began to find balance.

As a rule, if my use of technology leads me into deeper relationships with others, then I'm using it right. But if my use of technology creates distance or division from others, it's time to recalibrate.

Life in Airplane Mode

Be honest. How frequently do you rest? I'm not talking about a day of lying on the couch watching TV. I'm talking about silence, solitude, an untethered reprieve. It's tough, I know. With kids, friends, work, and countless other commitments, taking a whole day off seems unrealistic. So what does a life grounded in the Sabbath ethic look like? To begin with, it's more of a rhythm than a hard stop.

Let's turn our attention to where I'm sure it already is: your phone or other device. You likely have text messages, emails, and notifications waiting for you right now. A plethora of platforms and programs are begging you to pay attention to them. Yet at the same time, God whispers a subtle but compelling invitation to quiet and to peace. In this quiet peace, we can encounter him and re-center ourselves. Practice the rhythm of reaching for this quiet peace in the morning before you reach for your phone. When you have a break in your day, take the opportunity to practice silence and stillness rather than chasing the next distraction.

I first realized my need for committed rest when I started traveling a lot. Isolated on an airplane with no one I know and no Internet to connect to (although this is changing), I'm forced to enter silence and solitude. My brain quiets down, my body even falls right to sleep every time I take off in a plane. I eventually craved traveling because I wanted that beautiful peace I found on each flight. I wanted to put my life in Airplane Mode. Now, I spend evenings in Airplane Mode. I have to say no to invitations to hang out with friends, turn my phone off, and allow myself to quiet all the distractions in life. And I could easily make it seem like I'm really good at this one. But I'm not. It takes a lot of discipline and relational awareness to do this well.

The rhythm of a weekly day of rest is also something, as David and Jun noted earlier, that we tend to forget is included in the Ten Commandments. What's more, we forget its benefits for us, as well as its costs when we neglect to practice such rest. So go ahead — take a day off.

Take a Social Media Siesta

I have been working on small ways to detach myself from the ubiquitous Interwebz. One thing I have found helpful is to find something restful and peaceful to put me in a place where I have to detach from technology and action. If it is too difficult for me to turn off my phone for a day or two, I try getting away into an area where there is no cell phone signal. Contrary to popular belief, there are still areas of the United States that do not have a cell phone signal. Living in the Pacific Northwest, I have mountains, lakes, and trails just asking for me to go hiking and embark upon photo adventures. I grab a tent, my favorite people, and food for a couple of days. We find adventure and tranquility, and we create memories that are imprinted in our lives even more than on an Instagram photo. For me, my desire to create restful space in my life turned into something creative and active instead of inactive and absent.

Many of us who try this often return so refreshed that we can't remember why — or how — we have developed such a digital dependency in the first place. We are often unaware of our own dependency until we have an alternate experience with which to contrast it.

Reconsider Your Motives

Advertising companies are professionals with one common goal: how to decrease the friction a consumer sometimes feels between their desires and making the best decision. As consumers, we must consider which motives are behind our media decisions — and whether or not they're good ones.

The conversation in my head usually goes like this. "Brandon, consider your last Instagram upload or Facebook status. Are you counting the 'likes'? Are you gawking over the number of comments? Are you secretly harboring the hope of accumulating more affirmation and attention from your 'following'?"

Ask yourself the same questions sometime. Does the praise of others turn into a constant desire for positive feedback, causing you to act and make decisions based on pleasing people? I have to check my heart constantly as I look at the ways I communicate with real people on the other end of social media.

Then there's the question of immediate access. Ever since Amazon created the world of one-click purchasing, I can have the clothes I want when I want, that new TV series as soon as it is available for download, and the latest gadget delivered to my doorstep — all with a few clicks of a mouse or taps on a smartphone screen. But is this instant access driving purchasing decisions I wouldn't ordinarily make? Am I ingraining new habits just "because I can"?

Technology use in our lives is pervasive, yet it's not often critically considered. These are the questions that can help us take the pulse on the real reasons we're going hyperlinked and whether or not they're healthy reasons.

Pressing the reset button on a regular basis is the only way to recalibrate areas of our lives in which we may have unconscious dependencies. Technology is no exception.

I live in a hyperlinked world. That reality isn't going to go away anytime soon. I want to figure out how to live well in this world, how to be a disciple of Jesus in this complex culture. Following Jesus doesn't mean I have to throw away my iPhone and commit to a life without any digital tools. At the same time, I don't get a license to freely consume the world around me just because the tools I'm given enable me to do that more often and more efficiently.

Instead, I feel called to live in the tension between the two extremes. I want to live aware of how I am (or am not) honoring God, others, and myself through technology. These are some of the practices that have helped me along the way. I'd encourage you to try some of them for yourself and figure out some of your own. Let's remove our hyperlinks. ◆

Brandon Schulz is the co-founder of Comr.se. He has experience working with Fortune 500 companies and speaking across the US about the challenges facing his generation. A student of people and culture, Brandon lives in Seattle, WA, and finds ways to craft a life in a meaningful way.

AFTER YOU READ

- When you think of the hyperlinked life, what are you grateful for? What positive ways has it impacted your life?

- What about the hyperlinked life are you not so happy about? What costs do you feel you are paying in your own daily life?

- Which two or three "digital Sabbath" practices most appealed to you? How could you begin to practice those for yourself in the next month?

- How would you describe the persona or lifestyle you exhibit online? Also ask someone else to describe how you present yourself online. Find out what they think.

- What are some characteristics of the online person you *want* to be? How could you take steps to be more like this person—to reveal in your digital life the fruits of the Spirit and the gifts God has given you?

- When you think of being a steward of technology or information, what might that look like in your own life?

- Who can you mentor or be a role model for when it comes to navigating the hyperlinked life?

SHARE THIS FRAME

Who else needs to know about this trend?
Here are some tools to engage with others.

SHARE THE BOOK

• Any one of your friends can sample a FRAME for FREE.
  Visit zondervan.com/ShareFrames to learn how.

• Know a ministry, church, or small group that would benefit
  from reading this FRAME? Contact your favorite bookseller, or
  visit Zondervan.com/buyframes for bulk purchasing information.

SHARE THE VIDEOS

• See videos for all 9 FRAMES on barnaframes.com and use
  the share links to post them on your social networks and share
  them with friends.

SHARE ON FACEBOOK

• Like facebook.com/barnaframes and be the first to see new
  videos, discounts, and updates from the Barna FRAMES team.

SHARE ON TWITTER

• Start following @barnaframes and stay current with the
  trends that are influencing and changing our culture.

• Join the conversation and include #barnaframes whenever
  you post a FRAMES related idea or culture-shaping trend.

SHARE ON INSTAGRAM

• Follow instagram.com/barnaframes for sharable visual
  posts and infographics that will keep you in the know.

ABOUT THE RESEARCH

FRAMES started with the idea that people need simple, clear ideas to live more meaningful lives in the midst of increasingly complex times. To help make sense of culture, each FRAME includes major public opinion studies conducted by Barna Group.

If you're into the details, the research behind *The Hyperlinked Life* FRAME included 1,086 surveys conducted among a representative sample of adults over the age of 18 living in the United States. The survey was conducted from May 10, 2013, through May 20, 2013. The sampling error for this survey is plus or minus 3 percentage points, at the 95% confidence level.

If you're really into the research details, find more at www.barnaframes.com.

ABOUT BARNA GROUP

In its thirty-year history, Barna Group has conducted more than one million interviews over the course of hundreds of studies and has become a go-to source for insights about faith and culture. Currently led by David Kinnaman, Barna Group's vision is to provide people with credible knowledge and clear thinking, enabling them to navigate a complex and changing culture. The company was started by George and Nancy Barna in 1984.

Barna Group has worked with thousands of businesses, nonprofit organizations, and churches across the country, including many Protestant and Catholic congregations and denominations. Some of its clients have included the American Bible Society, CARE, Compassion, Easter Seals, Habitat for Humanity, NBC Universal, the Salvation Army, Walden Media, the ONE Campaign, SONY, Thrivent, US AID, and World Vision.

The firm's studies are frequently used in sermons and talks. And its public opinion research is often quoted in major media outlets, such as *CNN*, *USA Today*, the *Wall Street Journal*, Fox News, *Chicago Tribune*, the *Huffington Post*, the *New York Times*, *Dallas Morning News*, and the *Los Angeles Times*.

Learn more about Barna Group at www.barna.org.

THANKS

Even small books take enormous effort.

First, thanks go to Jun Young for his fine work on this FRAME—offering his years of experience and masterful communication skills to create what we pray is a prophetic and practical text to help us all navigate the realities of our hyperlinked lives.

We are also incredibly grateful for the practical contribution of Brandon Schulz, who is carefully navigating this "hyperlinked life" within his community.

Next, Barna Group gratefully acknowledges the efforts of the team at HarperCollins Christian Publishing, especially Chip Brown and Melinda Bouma for catching the vision from the get-go. Others at HarperCollins who have made huge contributions include Jennifer Keller, Kate Mulvaney, Mark Sheeres, and Shari Vanden Berg.

The FRAMES team at Barna Group consists of Elaina Buffon, Bill Denzel, Traci Hochmuth, Pam Jacob, Clint Jenkin, Robert Jewe, David Kinnaman, Jill Kinnaman, Elaine Klautzsch, Stephanie Smith, and Roxanne Stone. Bill and Stephanie consistently made magic out of thin air. Clint and Traci brought the research to life—along with thoughtful analysis from Ken Chitwood. And Roxanne deserves massive credit as a shaping force on

FRAMES. Amy Duty did heroic work on FRAMES designs, from cover to infographics.

Finally, others who have had a huge role in bringing FRAMES to life include Brad Abare, Justin Bell, Jean Bloom, Patrick Dodd, Grant England, Esther Fedorkevich, Josh Franer, Jane Haradine, Aly Hawkins, Kelly Hughes, Steve McBeth, Geof Morin, Jesse Oxford, Beth Shagene, and Santino Stoner.

Many thanks!

NOTES

1. Neil Postman, "Informing Ourselves to Death" (speech, German Informatics Society, Stuttgart, October 11, 1990).

2. *Business Insider*, February 7, 2013, http://www.businessinsider.com/15-billion-smartphones-in-the-world-22013-2.

3. *Foreign Affairs*, May/June 2013, http://www.foreignaffairs.com/articles/139104/kenneth-neil-cukier-and-viktor-mayer-schoenberger/the-rise-of-big-data.

4. IBM, http://www-01.ibm.com/software/data/bigdata/.

5. Archibald Hart and Sylvia Hart Frejd, *The Digital Invasion: How Technology is Shaping You and Your Relationships* (Grand Rapids: Baker Books, 2013), 149.

6. Royal Pingdom, "Internet 2012 in numbers," January 16, 2013, http://royal.pingdom.com/2013/01/16/internet-2012-in-numbers/.

7. Hart and Frejd, *The Digital Invasion*, 149.

8. AppAdvice, "The Number of Apps Downloaded Each Day Reaches 30 Million," January 20, 2011, http://appadvice.com/appnn/2011/01/number-apps-downloaded-day-reaches-30-million.

9. Skype Blog, "Thanks for Making Skype a Part of Your Daily Lives — 2 Billion Minutes a Day!," April 3, 2013, http://blogs.skype.com/2013/04/03/thanks-for-making-skype-a-part-of-your-daily-lives-2-billion-minutes-a-day/.

10. Royal Pingdom, "Internet 2012 in numbers," January 16, 2013, http://royal.pingdom.com/2013/01/16/internet-2012-in -numbers/.

11. Hart and Frejd, *The Digital Invasion*, 149.

12. Barna Group, *Family and Technology Report*, 2011.

13. Barna Group, "How the Last Decade Changed American Life," May 23, 2011, https://www.barna.org/family-kids-articles/ 488-how-technology-is-influencing-families.

14. Pew Research Center, *Just in Time Information*, May 7, 2012, http://pewInternet.org/Reports/2012/Just-in-time.aspx.

15. Mary Meeker, "Internet Trends Report," All Things D, May 2013, http://allthingsd.com/20130529/mary-meekers-Internet -trends-report-is-back-at-d11-slides/.

16. Cisco, *The Cisco Connected World Technology Report*, September 21, 2011.

17. Reported by News.com.au, June 2, 2013, http://www.news .com.au/technology/nomophobia-the-fear-of-not-having-a-mobile -phone-hits-record-numbers/story-e6frfro0-1226655033189.

18. Ted Thornhill, "Apps have overtaken the Web in popularity according to the latest statistics (actually, there's probably an app to tell you that)," *Daily Mail*, March 23, 2012, http://www .dailymail.co.uk/sciencetech/article-2119332/Apps-overtaken -Web-popularity-according-latest-statistics-actually-theres -probably-app-tell-that.html.

19. The Flurry Blog, April 3, 2013, http://blog.flurry.com/bid/ 95723/Flurry-Five-Year-Report-It-s-an-App-World-The-Just-Web -Lives-in-It.

20. IDC, *Worldwide and U.S. Mobile Applications, Storefronts, and Developer 2010–2014 Forecast and Year-End 2010 Vendor Shares:*

The "Appification" of Everything, December 2010, http://www.idc
.com/research/viewdocsynopsis.jsp?containerId=225668.

21. Videos of the Microsoft Envisioning Center are available on
YouTube.

22. See http://www.google.com/glass.

23. See http://research.microsoft.com/cue/skinput.

24. David Levy, *Love and Sex with Robots: The Evolution of
Human-Robot Relationships* (New York: Harper Perennial, 2007).

25. Nicholas Carr, *The Shallows: What the Internet Is Doing to Our
Brains* (New York: Norton, 2011), 116.

26. Neil Postman, *Amusing Ourselves to Death* (New York: Penguin,
1986).

27. CNN, "5 warning signs of gaming addiction," August 6,
2012, http://www.cnn.com/2012/08/05/tech/gaming-gadgets/
gaming-addiction-warning-signs.

28. Hart and Frejd, *The Digital Invasion,* 149.

29. See http://highlig.ht.

30. Sherry Turkle, *Alone Together: Why We Expect More from
Technology and Less from Each Other* (New York: Basic Books,
2011), xxi.

31. See http://www.praylive.com; http://www.24hourprayer
.com/; http://www.cbn.com/spirituallife/PrayerAndCounseling
/index.aspx#prayer.

32. Turkle, *Alone Together,* 293.

33. Peter Drucker, "The Next Society," *The Economist,* November 1,
2001, http://www.economist.com/node/770819.

Share Your Thoughts

With the Author: Your comments will be forwarded to the author when you send them to *zauthor@zondervan.com*.

With Zondervan: Submit your review of this book by writing to *zreview@zondervan.com*.

Free Online Resources at
www.zondervan.com

Daily Bible Verses and Devotions: Enrich your life with daily Bible verses or devotions that help you start every morning focused on God. Visit www.zondervan.com/newsletters.

Free Email Publications: Sign up for newsletters on Christian living, academic resources, church ministry, fiction, children's resources, and more. Visit www.zondervan.com/newsletters.

Zondervan Bible Search: Find and compare Bible passages in a variety of translations at www.zondervanbiblesearch.com.

Other Benefits: Register to receive online benefits like coupons and special offers, or to participate in research.

ZONDERVAN®